Friends

Hair Braiding

Friendship and Hair Braiding

This is a Parragon Publishing Book
First published in 2003

Parragon Publishing
Queen Street House
4 Queen Street
Bath BA1 1HE, UK

Written and Produced by
Caroline Repchuk
Art: Heather Heyworth
Photography: David Ellwand
Hairstyling: Christine Taylor
Friendship Bracelets: Claire Keen

Printed and bound in China
ISBN 1-40541-639-4

1ntroduction

This guide to braiding gives you the know-how to make amazing friendship bracelets, and create fabulous looks with beads and braids for your hair.

Step-by-step instructions will show you how to make some fantastic bracelets to wear, or to give to your friends and family! And you can use the same techniques to create some cool accessories to use in the fabulous braided hairstyles.

So hold out your hand in friendship, grab your best buddy and have fun!

Remember to keep all beads and small parts out of the reach of babies and small children.

Contents

Friendship Bracelets

If you keep your equipment ready in a box, you can make friendship bracelets almost anywhere!

You Will Need: Scissors A Ruler Sticky Tape
A Clipboard—this is a good, portable surface to work on.
You could use a piece of thick card with a clothes pin at the top.
Floss—inexpensive to buy from fabric and craft stores.
Beads—available at craft stores.

The Basic Knot

You need to learn to tie this knot in two directions, to make many of the bracelets in this book.

Left-Loop

1. Knot two strings together and clip or tape them to your board. Hold string B tightly. Cross string A over string B, leaving a loop sticking out.

2. Pass string A under string B and through the loop. Gently pull it to make a knot. Slide the knot up to the top and pull it tight.

3. Repeat so you have a double knot. This is a complete left-loop knot.

Right-Loop

1. Hold string B tightly. Cross string A over string B, leaving a loop sticking out.

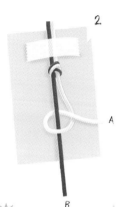

2. Pass string A under string B and through the loop. Gently pull it to make a knot. Slide the knot to the top and pull tight.

3. Repeat so you have a complete right-loop knot.

Hot Hints
Wrap a string around the wrist or ankle of the person your bracelet is for, and cut to size. Use as a guide so you know how long to make the bracelet.

Twister

This cool bracelet is the easiest to make—so get twistin'!
Choose three colors and cut three strings, 24in long.

1. Tie a knot 3in from the top, and tape the
strings to your board. Electrical tape from
hardware stores works well.

2. Hold the strings together
and, pulling firmly, twist them
until they feel tight.

3

3. Hold the twist firm with one
hand, and put a finger from your
other hand in the middle.
Now fold it in half, so
the ends meet.

Hot Hints
It's a good idea to use three different colors to start
as it makes the instructions easier to follow. Once you
feel confident, you can let your imagination run wild,
creating any color combination you like.

4. Hold the ends firmly. Remove your finger, and the twisted strings will quickly wind together, leaving a loop at one end.

5. Take the tape off and tie a knot in the free ends at the right length. Pull the knot through the loop to fasten. Hold the bracelet tight while you tie the knot or it will unwind.

Congratulations! You've made your first bracelet!

Hot Hints
Make a thicker bracelet by using more strings.
Add a large bead by pushing it over the looped end.

11

Basic Braid

This bracelet is so quick and easy, you can make one to match every outfit! Choose three colors and cut three lengths of each color, about 16in long.

1. Knot the strings at one end, and clip or tape them to your board.

A
B
C

A C B

2. Separate the colors, and spread them out in strands. Take strand C and cross it over strand B. Strand C is now in the middle.

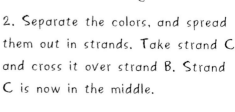

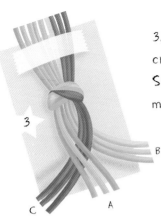

3. Now take strand A and cross it over strand C. Strand A is now in the middle.

B

C   A

4. Continue braiding in the same way, right over middle, left over middle, until the bracelet is long enough. Tie the ends in a knot, then fasten it on to your wrist.

B

C   A

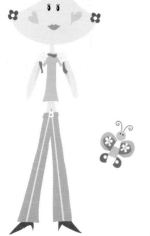

Hot Hints
As it is so quick and easy, this is a good pattern to choose if you want to make a long braid to wear as a headband, or around your belly.

13

Simple Stripes

This uses the basic left-loop knot, and is perfect for beginners! Choose three colors that blend or contrast well. Cut two lengths 28in long of each color.

1. Knot the six strings 3in from the top. Clip or tape them to your board. Set out as shown.

A B

A

2

B

2. Start with string A, and make a left-loop knot on string B, following the instructions on page 8. Remember to tie a double knot each time!

Hot Hints

Add beads by threading them on before the first or last knot of a row. Use the color of the stripes to help you space the beads evenly.

3. Using string A, continue making left-loop knots over each string, until you reach the end of the line. Leave string A on the right-hand side.

B   A

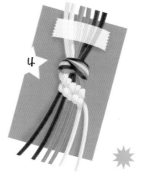

4

4. Now take string B, and make left-loop knots over each string across the line.

A   B

5. Keep going, using each string in turn, to make a pattern of repeating diagonal stripes.

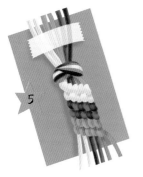

5

6. When the bracelet is long enough, tie the ends together in a knot, and trim them neatly with scissors.

15

Cupid's Arrow

Make this bracelet for someone you love! This pattern uses both left and right-hand knots. Choose four colors, and cut two strings in each color, 28in long.

1. Knot the strings about 3in from the top. Clip or tape them to your board. Set them out as shown.

A B C D E F G H

2. Use string A to make left-loop knots on strings B, C and D, following the instructions on page 8. Leave string A in the center.

B C D A E F G H

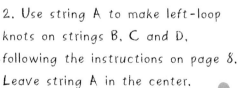

3. Now take string H and make right-loop knots on strings G, F and E. Leave string H in the center.

B C D A H E F G

16

4. Knot strings A and H together, using either a left or right-loop knot. This makes the point of the arrow.

B C D H A E F G

5

ABCD EFGH

5. Repeat from step 2 using the new outside strings, and knotting into the center. After four lines the strings will be back in their original position.

6. When the bracelet is long enough, tie a knot, and finish it by braiding the ends.

6

ABCDEFGH

Hot Hints
Add beads by threading them on to the outside string you are about to knot with. Make sure you have enough beads to complete your bracelet before you start.

Zig Zag

The fantastic zig zag shape of this bracelet is made by alternating knotting from left to right, and right to left! Choose four colors, and cut eight strings, each 36in long.

Hot Hints
Add a bead to accentuate each point.

1. Knot your strings 3in from the top, clip or tape them to your board. Set out the pairs of colors as shown.

1

2. Starting from the left, tie left-loop knots across the line. Continue with each string in turn to make double lines of each color.

3. Now starting on the right, tie right-loop knots across the line, and continue with the other strings as before.

4. Keep going until the bracelet is as long as you want. Tie off in a knot, then thread tiny beads on to each string, and knot off each string in turn.

Mermaids' Beads

This swirly bracelet has a spiral of knots running down it which look like beads. It looks fantastic—and it's very easy to make! You will need six strings in different colors, each 24in long.

1. Knot the strings 3in from the top. Tape them firmly to the edge of a table. (Check with a parent that it's ok)

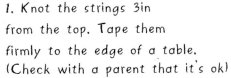

2. Take one string and hold the other five together in one strand. Make a left-loop knot over the other strings together and pull it up tightly.

20

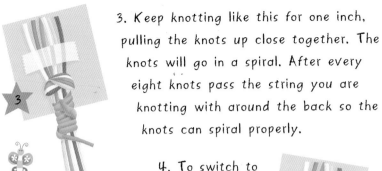

3. Keep knotting like this for one inch, pulling the knots up close together. The knots will go in a spiral. After every eight knots pass the string you are knotting with around the back so the knots can spiral properly.

4. To switch to another color, take out another string close to the last knot you made. Put the old string with the others, and continue knotting with the new string. Use each color in turn, and repeat to make a pattern.

5. When the bracelet is long enough, finish it by knotting and braiding the ends.

Hot Hints
This braid looks very pretty if you make it long enough to wear around your belly. Add beads to the bracelet before tying a knot, and do the next knot fairly loosely.

21

Broken Ladder

This beautiful bracelet looks complicated, but if you've tried making the Cupid's Arrow and Mermaids' Beads patterns, you will not find it too hard, as it combines the two!

Choose four colors. Cut two strings of each color, 28in long

1. Knot the strings 3in from the top and clip or tape them to your board. Set them out as shown.

2. Following the instructions on pages 16 and 17, knot the strings in the arrow pattern until you have used each color. The strings will be back in the order you started with.

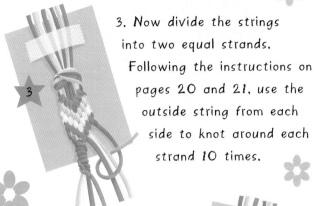

3. Now divide the strings into two equal strands. Following the instructions on pages 20 and 21, use the outside string from each side to knot around each strand 10 times.

4. Set out the strings again as shown. The outside strings you used to knot around the strands should now be in the center. Repeat the arrow pattern again, using each color.

5. Continue alternating the two patterns until the bracelet is long enough, then finish by knotting the ends.

Hot Hints
Practice the Cupid's Arrow and Mermaids' Beads patterns before trying this bracelet.

23

Going Loopy

Just two colors are needed to make this pretty bracelet. You will need four lengths 12in long for the center color, and four lengths 24in long to tie in loopy knots around the outside.

Hot Hints
This bracelet looks best when you use a dark color for the center strings, and a lighter color for the outside ones.

1. Knot the strings and clip or tape them to your board. Set them out with the shorter strings in the center, and a pair of the longer strings on each side, which you will work with as one strand.

1

A   B

2. Take strand A, and cross it over the center strings, leaving a loop on the left. Pass strand A under strand B.

A

2

B

3

B

A

3. Now pass strand B under strand A and the center strings, pull it through the loop on the left side, and over strand A. Slide the knot to the top.

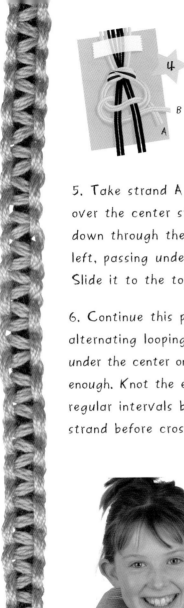

4. Strand A and B have switched sides. Take strand B, and pass it under the center strings and over strand A, leaving a loop on the left side.

5. Take strand A and cross it over the center strings and down through the loop on the left, passing under strand B. Slide it to the top.

6. Continue this pattern, alternating looping the outside strands over and under the center ones, until the bracelet is long enough. Knot the ends to finish. Add beads at regular intervals by slipping them on to the outside strand before crossing it over the center strings.

Starry Night

Follow the instructions carefully, and this starry pattern is not as hard as it looks! Cut four lengths of one color, 36in long. Cut two lengths of two other colors, 32in long.

1. Knot the strings, clip or tape them to your board, and set them out as shown.

ABCD EFGH

2. Following the instructions on pages 16 and 17, tie left and right-loop knots to make an arrow pattern, until you have four lines.

A B C D E F G H

3. Use string A to make a left-loop knot on string B. Use string H to make a right-loop knot on string G.

A B   G H

Hot Hints
Slip the floss onto a large needle, to make it easier to slide the beads on.

4. Using the center strings, knot the right one over all the strings to the right, using left-loop knots. Use the left one to knot all the strings to the left, using right-loop knots.

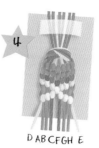

D AB CFGH E

5. Knot the new center strings together. Repeat step 4, working out from the center, until you have completed four lines, and the strings are back in their original position.

A BCD EFG H

6. Knot the center strings together. Knot the right center string over the next string, using a left-loop knot. Knot the left center string over the next string, using a right-loop knot. Knot the new center strings together.

AB DCFEGH

The center colors have switched over.

7. Continue following steps 2-6 until the bracelet is long enough. Tie a knot, add a small bead to each string, and tie off.

Take Care of Your Hair

Lustrous locks need love and attention, so whether your hair's long or short, straight or curly, blond or brunette, give it the TLC it deserves!

Washing your hair too often strips it of its natural oils. Use a product suited to your hair type, and switch brands from time to time, to prevent build-up on your hair.

Most styles are easier to do, and look better, on hair that has been washed a day or two before.

Your hair will grow longer and stronger if it is trimmed regulary—every 6 weeks if possible!

Don't use a brush on wet hair, or you could damage it. Comb it through, gently removing any tangles by holding your hair at the roots, and working up from the ends.

Adding Beads

Here's how to add beads to some of the braided styles that follow:

You will need beads, a hair threader and bead stoppers, all available from department stores.

1. Secure the end of a small braid with a bobby pin. Slide your beads on to a plastic hair threader.

2. Take off the bobby pin, and pass the end of the braid through the loop of the threader.

3. Push the beads toward the braid, and pull on the threader, until the braid is pulled through the beads.

4. Push a bead stopper into the last bead.

29

Ponytail

A ponytail keeps your hair neat, tidy and
off your face, and stops it from getting tangled.
It also forms the basis of many other styles.

1. Brush your hair, removing any tangles by holding your hair
at the roots, and gently working up from the ends.

2. Put a hair band over your
wrist, gather your hair at the
back of your head, and hold it
in the hand with the band..

3. Using the other hand, slip the
band off your wrist and over the
ponytail.

4. Twist the band and pull the
ponytail back through as many
times as you need to, until the
band is tight.

Flipover

For an extra twist, you can flip your ponytail over using a tool called a styler.

1. Gently push the pointed end into the hair, above the center of the band.

2. Push your ponytail through the loop, then pull the styler down, and your ponytail will flip over. If your hair is long enough, you could finish it off with a braid, following the instructions on pages 32 and 33.

Hot Hints
Never use rubber bands to secure your hair as they will damage it. Always use proper hair bands or scrunchies. Gather hair together on the top of your head for a high ponytail. Make it even more dynamic by securing it with several bands or scrunchies.

✹ Beautiful Braids ✹

Once you get the hang of
braiding it's very
easy. Braids of
different sizes can
be used to create all
kinds of funky styles!

1. Start by parting your hair down
the center. Using the hair on one
side, divide it into three equal
strands. Hold one outside section
in each hand.

2. Cross the back strand over the center strand,
taking hold of it with the other hand, and using your
fingers to keep the strands separate.

3. Now cross the front strand over the center strand, passing it to the other hand, again using your fingers to keep the strands separate.

4. Continue braiding, back to center, front to center, until you reach the end, then secure with a hair band. Repeat with the hair on the other side of your head.

Hot Hints
It may help to practice on a friend until you've got the hang of it!
Tie friendship braids around the hair bands for a really special finishing touch.

Party Girl

This style works best with long hair. It takes a while, so find a friend to help, or your arms may end up sore!

1. Brush your hair, and secure it with  a hair band on the top of your head, in a high ponytail.

2. Divide your ponytail into six equal sections, held with bobby pins.

Divide one section into three and braid it following the instructions on pages 32 and 33. Repeat with each section.

3. Now hold five of the braids in one hand, and wind the sixth braid around the base of the ponytail with your other. Secure it in place with hairpins.

4. Decorate the ends of your braids with ribbons or beads. Get set to party!

34

Braid Parade

Small beaded braids look fantastic framing your face.

1. Make a straight parting with a comb across your head from ear to ear. Secure the back section of your hair in a high ponytail.

2. Make a center parting in the front section of your hair and divide each

side into equal sections to braid around your face. Finish each braid with beads, following the instructions on page 29.

3. As an alternative to leaving all the braids hanging, you could sweep some up into your ponytail.

Hot Hints
Try to keep the beads on your braids at the same level. Choose colored beads to match your outfit.

Hippy Chick

This groovy hairstyle is very easy, and a great way to show off your friendship braids!

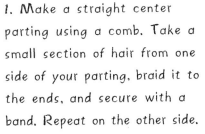

1. Make a straight center parting using a comb. Take a small section of hair from one side of your parting, braid it to the ends, and secure with a band. Repeat on the other side.

2. Take the braids around to the back of your head, and secure them together with a hair band. Release the bands at the ends of the braids, and unravel them up to the band at the top. Tie a friendship braid around to cover the band.

3. Braid two more sections of
hair in front of each ear, and
finish with beads, following
the instructions on page 29.

Hot Hints
Short on time? Secure the
top section of your hair
in a ponytail and slip on
a hippy headband!

Do the Twist

This stunning style looks really neat. It works well on short hair too, so is good if your hair is not long enough to braid.

1. Using a comb, part your hair into six sections across the front of your head. Clip each section together.

2. Take one section and twist it round and round tightly, right to the roots, pulling it back as you do so. Secure the twist with a butterfly clip.

3. Repeat with the remaining sections, working across your head.

4. Jazz up with as many decorations as you like. Clip-on beads, like the ones used here, work really well attached to each twist.

Hot Hints
Wrap a Twister friendship braid around the spirals for an extra fashion twist in the tale!

Spinning Spirals

This works well with shoulder-length or longer hair, and looks fun whether your hair is straight or curly.

1. Divide your hair into three sections across the top of your head.

2. As before, twist your hair tightly until it starts to spiral. Eventually it will curl right around itself and into a tight knot.

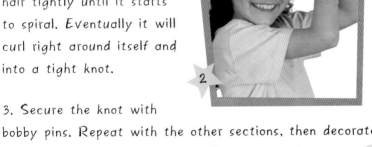

3. Secure the knot with bobby pins. Repeat with the other sections, then decorate with butterfly clips and sparkly hair accessories.

It's a Wrap

You'll need a friend for this! Take it in turns to do each other's hair, and soon you'll both be turning heads!

1. Cut three strings of different colored floss, twice the length of the hair you are going to wrap. Take a strand of hair, place it in the center of the strings and knot them on tightly, close to the roots.

2. Hold the strand of hair away from the head. Take one of the strings and wind it tightly round and round the hair and the other strings as neatly as you can.

3. After an inch, switch to another color. Keep alternating the colors until you reach the end of the strand.

4. Add some beads at the end, and secure by tying off the strings in a knot.

Hot Hints
If you don't have time to wrap your hair, try pinning or clipping in some friendship braids.

41

French Braid

French braids look so sleek and sophisticated, that it's worth taking time to practice, to get a really neat finish. For the best results, try and find someone to do it for you! Shoulder-length hair looks fantastic braided down each side.

1. Make a straight center parting using a comb. Starting at the front, divide your hair into three sections.

2. Braid left over center, right over center, as before.

3. Take up another loose section of hair from the left and add it to the left section as you braid it. Do the same on the right side.

4. Braid again, left over center, right over center. Stop to gather more hair into each outside strand and braid once more.

5. Keep braiding over your ear and down the side of your head, gathering in more hair as you go.

6. By the time you reach the nape of your neck, all of your hair should have been gathered into the three strands. Continue braiding to the ends and fasten with a hair band.

Hot Hints
Try adding some beaded hairpins for an even prettier finish to this style.

Braidy Bunch

These bouncy bunches will put a spring in your step!

1. Part your hair in the center. Divide off small sections and braid them as before, securing the ends with small bands. You will not be braiding all your hair, so hold the loose hair out of the way with a clip.

2. Gather together the loose hair and the braided hair on each side, and secure in two bunches.

3. Take one of the braids and wrap it around the base of each bunch, and secure it in place with hairpins. Finish by wrapping braided friendship bracelets around the end of each braid, and tying off securely.

45

Racy Ribbons

Long, straight hair will show off this style with the best effect, although it will work on shorter braids.

1. Divide your hair into small sections and braid it all over. You may need some help at the back. Secure the ends with small hair bands.

2. Take a piece of soft, narrow ribbon more than twice the length of the braid and fold it in half. Tie it to the top of the braid. Bind down the length of the braid, crossing the ribbon alternately at the front and back.

3. At the end of the braid, tie off the ribbons to cover the band and trim loose ends neatly. Continue with the rest of the braids. Alternatively, you could leave some braids without ribbons, and finish them by adding beads instead.

Hot Hints
Use multicolored ribbons if you're feeling really wacky, or color co-ordinate your braids to your outfit. Soft ribbons can be left in overnight as they won't pull your hair. As an alternative to ribbons, make some long Twister friendship braids, to wrap around your braids in the same way.

You Go Girls!